LOSING RELIGION, FINDING JESUS
Moving beyond Cultural Christianity

MATTHEW E. FERRIS

LUCIDBOOKS

Losing Religion, Finding Jesus
Moving beyond Cultural Christianity

Copyright © 2019 by Matthew E. Ferris

Published by Lucid Books in Houston, TX
www.LucidBooksPublishing.com

All rights reserved. No part of this publication may be reproduced, stored in a retrieval system, or transmitted in any form by any means, electronic, mechanical, photocopy, recording, or otherwise, without the prior permission of the publisher, except as provided for by USA copyright law.

ISBN-10: 1-63296-363-9
ISBN-13: 978-1-63296-363-5
eISBN-10: 1-63296-349-3
eISBN-13: 978-1-63296-349-9

Unless otherwise indicated, Scripture quotations are taken from the ESV® Bible (The Holy Bible, English Standard Version®), copyright © 2001 by Crossway, a publishing ministry of Good News Publishers. Used by permission. All rights reserved.

Scripture quotations marked (GNT) are taken from the Good News Bible © 1994 published by the Bible Societies/HarperCollins Publishers Ltd UK, Good News Bible© American Bible Society 1966, 1971, 1976, 1992. Used with permission.

Scripture quotations marked (NASB) are taken from the New American Standard Bible® (NASB), Copyright © 1960, 1962, 1963, 1968, 1971, 1972, 1973, 1975, 1977, 1995 by The Lockman Foundation. Used by permission. www.Lockman.org.

Scripture quotations marked (NIV) are taken from the Holy Bible, New International Version®, NIV®. Copyright ©1973, 1978, 1984, 2011 by Biblica, Inc.™ Used by permission of Zondervan. All rights reserved worldwide. www.zondervan.com. The "NIV" and "New International Version" are trademarks registered in the United States Patent and Trademark Office by Biblica, Inc.™

Special Sales: Most Lucid Books titles are available in special quantity discounts. Custom imprinting or excerpting can also be done to fit special needs. Contact Lucid Books at Info@LucidBooksPublishing.com.

Table of Contents

Cultural Christianity	1
Imitation Gospels	9
God's Blueprint	15
Missing the Mark	23
The Love of God	31
The Wrath of God	37
Turning from Sin	45
Turning to God	51
Follow Me	59
That Your Joy May Be Full	67
Afterword	75
Notes	77

"Matt Ferris has a knack for discerning the essential truths of Scripture and Christian doctrine, simplifying them (without watering them down), and writing about them with both directness and charm."

—**William Ray**,
author of *Answered Prayer: The Jesus Plan*

"Matt Ferris has written an exceptional book for understanding cultural Christianity. In it, believers will find facts to explain what they've been seeing but haven't fully understood. Non-Christians will be directed to the Bible, examining how to fill the God-shaped hole they may or may not have recognized in their lives. As a pastor I appreciated the accurate biblical theology, but as a believer I enjoyed the encouraging, clearly thought out 'gut checks.' Read this book!"

—**Chris Fogle**,
author of *Biblical Knowledge, Understanding and Wisdom*

"Christianity is much more than morality, more than following a list of rules, more than doing the right things, more than making a profession of support for Jesus as for a sports team or a politician. It is a relationship with Jesus; he calls us to follow him, to find our identity and resources in him, to carry out his mission in the world as his ambassadors. In a readable and gracious style, Ferris contrasts cultural or nominal Christianity with the real thing. This is an excellent resource for new believers and those investigating the faith, but also for those who have been Christians a long time. Finding Jesus is not a one-time event but a lifelong process."

—**Glenn R. Kreider**,
professor of theological studies, Dallas Theological Seminary

Cultural Christianity

Whatever independence Americans believe they possess, they nevertheless view themselves as people of Christian faith. The 2014 Pew Religious Landscape Survey found that just over 70 percent of Americans identify with some branch of Christianity. Although this number has declined in recent years, it is still a healthy majority. But as one digs deeper into the findings, there is variation on commitment. The amount of people who say religion is very important in their lives drops to 53 percent, a decrease of 17 percent that demonstrates the cultural shift toward nominalism.[1] *Merriam-Webster* gives one definition of nominal as "existing or being something in name or form only."[2] When the name is there, but not the essence, when there is form, but a lack of substance, all that remains is nominalism.

In Name Only?
Consider someone who dismisses the idea that they follow their city's baseball team all that much, yet they hold season tickets, know the statistics of every player on the team, and never miss the broadcast of an away game. We would say that their actions make them a true fan, no matter what they say. Similarly, if someone else claims to be a huge fan, but can't remember the last time they went to a game or watched one on television, we would doubt whether they are that much of a fan. They are nominally a fan, but nothing beyond that.

When it comes to Christian faith, nominalism means much the same thing. There is a disconnect between what someone says and what someone does. One may be a Christian in name, but it is only in name, for there is a gulf between profession and practice. The Pew survey demonstrates nominalism with the statistic of the "frequency of participation in prayer, scripture study, or religious education groups by importance of religion." Only 42 percent say these activities are very important, a fair bit lower than the 70 percent who identify as Christian.[3] This shows a continuum from commitment to nominalism. If it is only in name, can someone truly claim the identity of being a Christian? To be a Christian is to be a disciple, a follower, but in nominal faith, there is not much following.

Nominalism isn't a recent or only a modern problem. In fact, we find it in the Bible. The book of Exodus describes how the Jewish nation experienced a mighty and miraculous liberation from slavery in Egypt. God brought judgment on the Egyptian Pharaoh and the whole land when he would not give the Israelites their freedom, an event marked by the Passover.

In the subsequent years, the people of Israel went through many trials, wars, defeats, and deliverance, but they also drifted away from God. The intimacy their forefathers enjoyed with him in those early days was gone. Unlike Abraham, who was called "the friend of God," they had become distant from him, and unlike Moses, who spoke with God directly, they had become strangers to him. The prophets decried this, as God spoke through Isaiah:

> "This people draw near with their mouth
> and honor me with their lips,
> while their hearts are far from me."
>
> —Isaiah 29:13

Israel, God's chosen people, had slipped into a cultural connection to God. By the time of Jesus, we can see this in full bloom. John the Baptist, speaking to the religious leaders of his day, gave this blunt warning about nominalism: "And do not presume to say to yourselves, 'We have Abraham as our father,' for I tell you, God is able from these stones to raise up children for Abraham" (Matt. 3:9).

John cautions them against trusting in pedigree. Whatever relationship their ancestors may have had with God is not important for their own, something that is true for everyone. Coming from good stock counts for nothing, nor does a "Judeo-Christian heritage."

With a cultural faith, it is particularly insidious because it comes with false assumptions. This, too, is what John warns of, when assumption becomes presumption. We can think all is well in our relationship with God, but there is nothing there, no reality or substance. Imagine setting out for a long-planned trip overseas. You've set the itinerary, booked hotels and airplane tickets, and taken care of everything. When you arrive at the airport, however, you have no passport! You aren't allowed to board the plane, and all your plans are scuttled. Arriving at the end of life without a genuine relationship with the Lord Jesus is like having no spiritual passport. This is the danger of a faith that is in name only.

It's not just fire and brimstone prophets of the Old Testament who spoke about the dangers of nominalism. Jesus himself gave these warnings several times. He calls religious leaders of his day "whitewashed tombs, which outwardly appear beautiful, but within are full of dead people's bones and all uncleanness" (Matt. 23:27).

In the last book of the Bible, Revelation, Jesus himself spoke messages to seven different churches, and the final letter, to the church in Laodicea, is not a message of consolation: "For you say, I am rich, I have prospered, and I need nothing, not realizing that you are wretched, pitiable, poor, blind, and naked" (Rev. 3:17).

Their own belief that they needed nothing indicates they felt pretty good about their spiritual condition, but despite what they thought, Jesus had a different view of the real state of their faith and lives. The other description of this church is "lukewarm." They are neither cold nor hot, and Jesus himself found this kind of attitude repulsive. "Because you are lukewarm, and neither hot nor cold, I will spit you out of my mouth" (Rev. 3:16).

A lukewarm relationship with God is a perpetual danger in every age, because every time faith is passed forward, this is a point where the next generation may not make it their own. The Lausanne Committee for World Evangelization describes a nominal believer as one who "would call himself a Christian, or be so regarded by others, but who has no authentic commitment to Christ based on personal faith. Such commitment involves a transforming personal relationship with Christ, characterized by such qualities as love, joy, peace, a desire to study the Bible, prayer, fellowship with other Christians, a determination to witness faithfully, a deep concern for God's will to be done on earth, and a living hope of heaven to come."[4] The ones Lausanne first identifies have not made faith in Christ their own, in contrast to the authentic believer.

The elements in this description are really twofold. On the one side, there is a claim to faith and a connection to Jesus Christ, and on the other, the features that come with having this relationship, but they are absent in the person of nominal faith. A cultural faith is about the external, a genuine faith is about the internal, a nominal faith is about doing, true faith is about being. The relationship that is real is transformational, not leaving us where we are, but making us new. A hallmark of cultural faith is a focus on behavior, on ensuring people are adhering to the rules. They may look good, just as Jesus told his hearers they "appeared beautiful." Inside, however, there was nothing that indicated a change had occurred, there was no life.

Cultural Christians believe that if the externals are all right, it means the internal transformation has taken place, or even that such an internal transformation is perhaps not so important. They are comfortable that if people are doing the things that good people do, that's what is most important. An internal change, being born again, isn't really significant. This is what puts cultural Christianity at odds with biblical faith.

The understanding of personal faith is likewise different with cultural believers. Personal faith often means they keep their faith to themselves, thinking it's not their place to foist it on anyone else. Personal faith for the true Christian means, as Lausanne indicates, a transformational relationship. Being born again is a description of this transformation.

Nicodemus Interviews Jesus

I recall overhearing a conversation years ago between two people who were speaking about faith. The one said to the other, "You're not one of those 'born-again' Christians, are you?" The question reveals a lot, most importantly that this person doesn't know the Bible very well. The term *born again* is not something that was invented by TV preachers or by the religious right. Jesus himself used these words when he talked with Nicodemus, a Jewish leader. Jesus likened faith in him to birth. Everyone experiences physical birth, but Jesus uses the metaphor of birth to speak about spiritual life. Physical life is conceived and a person is born. Spiritual life, too, is something that begins, and Jesus speaks of conversion in these terms because the picture compellingly shows the necessity of this spiritual birth.

Jesus tells Nicodemus, "Truly, truly, I say to you, unless one is born again he cannot see the kingdom of God" (John 3:3). You cannot be part of God's family without the new birth! In other words, the only way to have spiritual life is to be born again. It's redundant to speak about being "one of those born-again Christians," because that is the only kind of Christian there is. It is not possible to be in God's family unless you have been born again. Think about that for a moment, and ask yourself whether you have been born again. If you would be uncomfortable describing yourself with that term, it likely indicates cultural faith, and not Christian life.

Some may think that nominalism appears mostly in so-called mainline denominations: Methodists, Presbyterians, and other Protestant groups. But these groups were historically full of zealous believers, ablaze with passion for God. The Wesley brothers, John and Charles, were completely sold out to God, but their ecclesiastical descendants often bear a different character. No group, no tradition should feel that nominalism would never affect them. Even the most fervent, evangelical congregations are liable to nominalism. It is a kind of spiritual entropy no one is immune to.

One of the biggest dangers of cultural faith may be that, for many, it acts as a kind of inoculation. They are exposed to some part of faith and the gospel, but it's not a gospel that says "you must be born again." Rather, it's a gospel that says, "God loves you and wants you to be happy." The first part of that statement is true. God's love sent the Lord Jesus into the world to die on the cross. But the second part is deceptive.

We as human beings are exceedingly poor judges of what will make us happy. Just as Adam and Eve thought it would make them happy to eat of the tree in the middle of Eden, so we often choose what appeals to our own immediate desires, but our choices frequently bring us spiritual harm. We're conditioned to think that our happiness is the ultimate measure of our good, and that becomes the gauge we use to evaluate our decisions. "Well, what's most important is that you're happy." Personal experience and the Bible both testify against this.

When our minds are trained to think this way, and we encounter the gospel, we resist its message. We don't agree that we are all that bad, and we don't agree that we deserve God's wrath for our rebellion against him. The gospel begins with these truths drawn from Scripture. Cultural faith fashions a gospel that is comfortable and doesn't disturb a person's life. Faith is a good thing, to be sure, but one shouldn't get too carried away. Cultural faith doesn't make demands on a person, and it doesn't feel constrained by what the Bible says.

You may have cultural-only faith if:
- You think of yourself as a pretty good person.
- You believe God is forgiving toward those who are doing their best.
- You don't think all that often about your own sin or its consequences.
- You look to things like baptism, church membership, or church attendance as evidence of faith.
- You have family members who show no sign of knowing God, but you're not concerned about them.
- You would be offended if someone asked you if you have been saved.

There is nuance in some of these statements, and I'll explore them further for what they imply, but the most important point is that cultural faith is not saving faith. It doesn't bring a person from death to life, it doesn't bring salvation, and in the end, cultural faith is a soul-endangering counterfeit for the real thing. This is why the question is important, and why those who have only this kind of faith need deliverance from it.

If this describes you, I have been where you are. I had religion, but I did not have life. I can never remember a time in my life when I did not believe God exists. But I wasn't able to say, "And I know I have a relationship with him that cannot be broken." I was doing the things religion told me to do, but those things didn't bring pardon from the guilt of sin, and they didn't bring me into a relationship with the living God through his Son. Religion can look so much like the real thing that we can be fooled into thinking it is, but the differences are all-important.

Imitation Gospels

The market for knock-off consumer goods is large. A 2016 *Money* magazine article estimates the global worth of the industry at $461 billion dollars, about the size of the economy of Austria. Five percent of goods imported to Europe are fake.[1] Even though people know products from certain designers are costly, they still want to believe that what's before them is the real thing and that they are getting an incredible deal. That phenomenon operates in the area of Christian belief as well. There are parallels between knock-off consumer goods and the messages sometimes offered as the Christian gospel. Looking at these can help us spot where the fake is and how the real differs from it.

They Resemble the Real Thing
Imitation goods are specifically fashioned to look just like the real thing or very close to it. Who would want a Rolex that is easy to spot as a fake? The knock-off item looks like the genuine item or close enough that people are fooled, especially those not familiar with the true version. Perhaps it's a slight difference in the logo or in the materials, but there is always something that gives it away. When it comes to the gospel, cultural Christianity bears enough resemblance to the real thing that many can't tell the difference, but just as with knock-offs, once you start inspecting the details, the differences emerge that tell you it's not authentic.

Cultural Christianity says things like, "It's important to follow Jesus, and to live by the tenets of Christianity." But what does it mean to follow Jesus? If it means we go to church, we give money, and we strive to be better, these things sound commendable, but they aren't the true item. What's missing? Recall what Jesus told Nicodemus: "You must be born again" (John 3:7). The necessity of the new birth implicitly denies that things like attending church, trying to be good, or giving money in any way lead a person to becoming a new creature in Jesus Christ. The apostle Paul said, "If anyone is in Christ, he is a new creation. The old has passed away; behold, the new has come" (2 Cor. 5:17). The New Testament speaks of becoming a Christian in these contrasts of exchanging the old for the new, of passing through death to come to life, and of once being condemned but now forgiven. None of the things in the list of what many think of as being a Christian get at this reality of being made new in Christ.

In that same chapter, Paul goes on to say, "All this is from God, who through Christ reconciled us to himself and gave us the ministry of reconciliation; that is, in Christ God was reconciling the world to himself, not counting their trespasses against them, and entrusting to us the message of reconciliation" (2 Cor. 5:18–19). We need reconciliation because our natural state is that we are against God; we are, due to our sin, the enemies of God.

Indeed, one who is a new creature in Christ does follow Jesus and strives to demonstrate their identity in Christ by loving others, believers and unbelievers alike, and also giving of their money as an act of worship. But doing these things will not cause one to be born again. When cultural Christianity seems to mimic these things yet denies the problem of sin and the necessity of the death of Christ, it is an imitation of the real thing.

Cheaper Than the Genuine Article

When traveling in Asia, one sees a lot of outdoor markets where popular brands like Gucci and Coach are available for much cheaper than they are domestically. The reason is that Asia is the source of many knock-off goods. Usually the purchaser knows this and is buying something with a wink and a nod. If the purchase price is a fraction of what the authentic item sells for, it often indicates it's a fake.

A gospel that makes no claim on the believer, that says no repentance is needed and no real change comes with believing in Jesus, is a form of "much cheaper than the real thing." The true gospel is a call to repentance and faith that brings with it a break from the old. If you have always gone to church or have been baptized and confirmed, it can be difficult to see that you have just as much need as anyone to turn from sin and self. Being baptized as an infant is something done to you, not in you. Being confirmed as an adolescent is something done to you, not in you.

Religion and the imitation gospels tell people lies about themselves. "God loves you just as you are" is a half-truth because it implies that you can stay as you are; that is, in your sin and opposition to God. And we love to believe these half-truths! They require nothing from us because they don't confront us with our true condition, nor can they promise true change and true life.

Close to the end of his time on earth, Jesus prepared the twelve disciples for what was ahead. He told them plainly he would die on the cross, and because of their association with him, they would be persecuted. "If the world hates you, know that it has hated me before it hated you. If you were of the world, the world would love you as its own; but because you are not of the world, but I chose you out of the world, therefore the world hates you" (John 15:18–19).

Believers in Jesus expect to incur the hatred of the world—that part of humanity opposed to God. It comes as the cost of being a follower of him. A message that says there is no cost, no opposition, is an imitation gospel, one that portrays things differently from what the New Testament promises. That doesn't mean Christians should go around looking for a fight, ready to cry foul at any disagreement or slight, but it does mean that if a believer is modeling Christ-like behavior, he shouldn't be surprised if not everyone embraces him. To be sure, Jesus did not leave his disciples with no hope. On the contrary, he is the whole reason for their hope! "I have said these things to you, that in me you may have peace. In the world you will have tribulation. But take heart; I have overcome the world" (John 16:33). Overcoming the world means that no matter what happens, believers in Christ can experience peace. They have counted the cost of following him to be worth it because of the promises, not only of eternal life, but also of an abundant life here.

Despite what some television preachers may say, the abundant life Jesus spoke about does not mean magnificent wealth or freedom from trials. On the contrary, it is a life that, even in the midst of the same challenges every person faces, can experience contentment, because Christians have a different hope, a different outlook than those without Christ. Our sufferings are not empty, not without purpose. They are to conform us to Christ—an eternal purpose. While the imitation gospel says that God's purpose is to make us happy, the real thing says God's purpose is to make us holy, to make us like his Son.

Many people are quite ready to accept a message of God's grace. A message of pardon, freely given without our effort, without our good deeds—who wouldn't embrace that? But the gospel of Jesus Christ is twofold; it is both a call and a command. The call is to partake freely of the grace God offers in pardoning our sin. The command is that we turn from that sin. While preaching to the Athenians, the apostle Paul reaches the apex of his message with this: "The times of ignorance God overlooked, but now he commands all people everywhere to repent, because he has fixed a day on which he will judge the world in righteousness by a man whom he has appointed; and of this he has given assurance to all by raising him from the dead" (Acts 17:30–31).

In considering the cost of being a follower of Jesus, you should not fall into the trap of thinking that the depth of your sacrifice is what earns God's favor. The cost is not measured that way. Christians sometimes speak of the "finished work of Christ." This illustrates that salvation is based on the fact that Jesus died for our sins and rose again. Nothing we do contributes to that. My devotion or fervor adds nothing to his accomplishment at the cross and the empty tomb, but I can take away from it. If I seek to enhance it with my own penance or my own effort, I end up diminishing it. One cannot improve on what God has done. My response to what he has done is worship and discipleship; it is not my contribution to becoming a Christian or one day being in heaven.

Of Far Lower Worth in the End

Wolfgang Beltracchi is a German painter of remarkable talent. Rather than sell his paintings as his own, he decided he could make more money by forging famous artists, mostly of the early twentieth century. Beltracchi's work was so good that several high-profile art historians were tricked into certifying the fakes as original works. Many pieces were auctioned for millions, but when the truth of Beltracchi's artifice came out, these paintings were worth nowhere near what they had sold for.

With a gospel that is a forgery, the tragedy is that it is only when it is too late that the discovery comes that someone believed in what ultimately proved empty. The book of Hebrews says, "It is appointed for man to die once, and after that comes judgment" (Heb. 9:27). Popular culture has incorporated the first part as "you only live once," but they usually dismiss the second half. But as we saw from various passages in the Bible, judgment is a genuine promise from God, and it is only in this life that one can choose to follow the Lord. After death, it is too late. It will be only then that many realize the worth, or rather worthlessness of the cultural Christianity they had.

To go through all my life believing I am fulfilling an obligation and doing what God requires of me, only to find out that the object of my faith had no power to save, no message of redemption, and no deliverance from sin and its consequences, is catastrophic. This is why imitation gospels are so deceptive. They bear a passing resemblance to the real thing, and unless we look into God's Word for guidance, we will be like the art historian who was fooled.

The gospel of the Bible always makes much of Jesus and his work on the cross. The true gospel always presents the need of mankind to be pardoned from the guilt of our sin. The true gospel always makes much of the power of Jesus's blood to bring pardon for that sin and deliverance from the slavery of it, and the true gospel celebrates a risen savior, knowing that the resurrection is necessary for our salvation. The true gospel always presents our response to these facts as what determines whether we have true life, or just a cheap imitation. I encourage you to ask yourself honestly whether you've got the genuine article.

God's Blueprint

For over a decade, I worked in the Sears Tower in downtown Chicago. Until Malaysia's Petronas Towers displaced it in 1998, it was the tallest building in the world. The architectural firm of Skidmore, Owings & Merrill who designed the structure had the challenge of how to construct a building this tall yet ensure it was structurally sound. The plans for the building were no doubt exceedingly detailed and substantial. Imagine if the crews constructing the tower looked at the plans at the beginning but didn't refer back to them after that. What kind of result would they have gotten? Would the skyscraper match the blueprint? Would it even stand up?

A "Holey" Bible?

The relationship of the cultural Christian to the Bible is similar to this. Many acknowledge the Bible as important, or authoritative, but they don't read it with any regularity. If we believe we understand how God has designed salvation, but we are ignoring what the architect set down, will the result match the plans? In the previous chapter, I referenced several verses of Scripture. Throughout these pages I present a perspective that relies on the Bible as the final word in the truth of spiritual matters. There are two reasons for this. The first is that I believe the Scriptures of the Old and New Testaments to be God's true word, and that they are his message. Second, if you make any claim to Christian faith, in some sense, you also believe the Bible to be the Word of God. There is a myriad of views on the Scriptures, but it's not unusual in Western Christianity to find doubts about the truth of God's Word. Many say the Bible contains a message from God, but it is common to find those who affirm that the Bible likely contains some errors, or to question whether God verbally inspired the writers of Scripture.

These positions exclude one another. If I believe the Bible to be God's very word, I will not remain a cultural believer. If I am a cultural believer, one of the reasons for that is because of my attitude about the Bible. It isn't my purpose to convince you of the truth of the Scriptures. In my experience, the best method of that is when someone reads the Bible for herself. The Scriptures testify to their own truth and bear witness to a unity of purpose and to a single author. Anyone willing to read the Bible with some amount of seriousness and openness will see this.

Thomas Jefferson famously took a knife to his Bible, cutting out all those portions he doubted were true. He set aside all the miracles in the New Testament, and what remains is a book to encourage morality and good citizenship. He called this *The Life and Morals of Jesus of Nazareth*. Jefferson was left with a Bible that was literally full of holes; parts were missing. Many of us are like Jefferson. We may not physically cut pages out of the Bible, but we put them aside as untrue or dubious, and as a result, we don't feel bound to submit to what the Scriptures say.

But this is an inconsistent position. We know about the Lord Jesus from Scripture. We know about his suffering on the cross from Scripture, and we know about his resurrection from the dead from Scripture. Why would you believe these core truths of the Christian faith, yet other things found on the same pages of the gospels, you do not?

It is common to find someone raising doubts about the Bible for its alleged inconsistencies, but this objection is almost always not the real concern. Paul Little was a Christian worker who traveled around university campuses in the mid-twentieth century presenting the truth of Christianity. He noted that it was common in his question-and-answer sessions to have someone ask, "What about all the contradictions in the Bible?" Little replied, "It is good to ask the questioner what errors he has in mind. Often there are none, and it is evident that he hasn't even read the Bible."[1]

The underlying reason many say they do not believe the Scriptures is very rarely an intellectual one or that the evidence doesn't support belief. Rather, the overwhelming reason people doubt the Scriptures is because God's Word makes a claim on them. If what the Bible says about Jesus Christ, sin, and judgment are true, then I must do something with these truths. But if I hold the claims of Scripture at a distance and say, "I'm just not sure, I have my doubts," then I absolve myself of responsibility to take a stand on the claims of the Lord Jesus Christ (or at least I think I do).

Do you read the Bible, respect the Bible, and believe it is a holy book? Do you think it contains God's Word and his truth, but you are not convinced of all that it says? Do you affirm those parts of the Bible that speak of God's love, but dismiss those that speak of coming judgment? If you believe in God, you attend church, and do those things that are associated with Christian belief, yet your attitude toward the Scriptures is to be skeptical of their truthfulness, this is a problematic position for you. All the practices you participate in are biblically based, and thus you are picking and choosing, giving some credence to the Bible, but not all credence. On what basis do you make those decisions?

That's Your Interpretation

My previous statement about the Bible as the final word may have you asking, "But whose interpretation of the Bible?" Indeed, this is one of the more frequent reasons used to dismiss a claim of biblical truth: "That's your interpretation." I don't gloss over the issue by saying that the Bible doesn't have difficult passages, but there are other parts of Scripture that are so clear it takes real effort to misunderstand them. The core beliefs of the Christian faith are among the second category.

One cannot read the New Testament without seeing that Jesus claimed to be God. "I and the Father are one," he told his audience (John 10:30). Nor can we misunderstand that Jesus also affirmed he is the only way of salvation. "I am the way, and the truth, and the life. No one comes to the Father except through me" (John 14:6). Similarly, the certainty of life after death and the reality of hell are doctrines Jesus preached about repeatedly. I could cite other passages of Scripture to demonstrate that the claims Jesus and his apostles made are not nebulous or confusing. Salvation through Jesus Christ alone is not a matter of interpretation.

Still, it is obvious that some traditions dismiss these things, but they do so only by the most labored of Scripture reading. (I'll examine a number of these things in the following pages.) If we bring our own ideas, or the ideas of others, and import these as a grid to lay on top of God's Word, we can certainly rationalize a view of the Bible that dismisses its authority, but we do so at our own spiritual peril. What confidence can one have in saying that those parts of the New Testament that speak of hell are fiction or not to be taken literally, while at the same time asserting that anything that speaks of God's love for humanity is absolutely trustworthy?

Any approach to the Bible should encompass several things and avoid others. It isn't unusual to find readers of Scripture treating it as a handbook for living, prescribing how we should live, and conversely warning us about what we should not do. But this is deceptive. Conversion to Jesus Christ and new life in him is not a behavior modification program. It's not a formula for "your best life now." In fact, the first Christians became followers of Jesus at great cost to themselves. Many were tortured and killed. Treating the Bible as a handbook for living appears to honor God, but in fact it is a backdoor method of affirming ourselves as the center of God's plan.

The Bible is ultimately a message about Jesus Christ. He is the central theme running through both the Old and New Testaments. If we say we have a relationship with him while we are doubtful about his word to us, it puts us in a position of authority over him. Perhaps you haven't thought about it in this way before, but if you cast parts of Scripture aside as unreliable, or historically inaccurate, you are doing just that.

A Claim of Truth Exclusive of All Others

It has become popular to assess spiritual truth in a way that at first appears open-minded, and affirms that our understanding is limited. For example, someone might say, "No one religion has all the truth. Each has portions that are true." Timothy Keller comments on the illustration of blind men feeling their way around an elephant as an example. "Several blind men were walking along and came upon an elephant that allowed them to touch and feel it. 'This creature is long and flexible, like a snake,' said the first blind man, holding the elephant's trunk. 'Not at all—it is thick and round like a tree trunk,' said the second blind man, feeling the elephant's leg. 'No, it is large and flat,' said the third blind man, touching the elephant's side. Each blind man could only feel part of the elephant—none could envision the entire elephant. In the same way, it is argued, the religions of the world each have a grasp on part of the truth about spiritual reality, but none can see the whole elephant or claim to have a comprehensive vision of the truth."[2]

Taking a position that recognizes the limits of our finite minds sounds reasonable and humble. But Keller points out the flaw in this. "This illustration backfires on its users. The story is told from the point of view of someone who is not blind. How could you know that each blind man only sees part of the elephant unless *you* claim to be able to see the whole elephant?"[3]

Our difficulty in understanding parts of Scripture is a different thing. Every reader of the Bible acknowledges this. Those with more than a passing familiarity with the Bible recognize that we need to hold some positions in humility, admitting that we don't yet fully comprehend some parts of God's Word. We continue to read and to study these parts, seeking a surer grasp of God's truth. Some take a different stance, stating that because some parts of Scripture do not make sense to us now, they must be in error. This is shortsighted. Imagine if someone were to pronounce a textbook on physics wrong because all parts did not make sense on the first reading. This is not an uncommon attitude toward God's Scriptures. Whether it is a lack of understanding that the Middle Eastern culture was the cradle of God's Word, or failing to see the overarching themes of the Bible, some readers of Scripture throw up their hands at the hard parts and say, "It must be wrong."

It's important as well to see that God's Word contains promises about itself. Psalm 19, for example, testifies to the trustworthiness of the Bible.

> The commandment of the LORD is pure,
> enlightening the eyes;
> the fear of the LORD is clean, enduring forever;
> the rules of the LORD are true,
> and righteous altogether.
>
> —Psalm 19:8–9

Purity, truth, and eternity are all hallmarks of God's Word. Recalling Jesus's words that he is the only way to God—this is a claim of exclusivity. No one comes to God except through him. This claim of exclusivity is there throughout the Scriptures. In the New Testament, Paul speaks of Scripture as "God-breathed" (2 Tim. 3:16). That is, God himself breathed out these words. If we believe he can give us eternal life, do we not believe the Word that tells us about that life? Finally, Jesus himself made the following statement about his own teaching. "If anyone's will is to do God's will, he will know whether the teaching is from God or whether I am speaking on my own authority" (John 7:17). In other words, our attitude is key. Are we teachable, and do we desire to follow after what God has told us? If so, this goes a long way to answering any questions of the reliability of the Bible. To understand the Bible, we must begin by reading it with open hearts.

It may not be opposition to the Bible, but simply unfamiliarity and ignorance of it that mark a person's relationship to Scripture. In many churches, there is a weekly reading of a few passages of Scripture, but not much beyond this. In some congregations, reading of the Bible for oneself, trying to grasp the whole of God's message from Genesis to Revelation, is not encouraged. That is left to the clergy, and it's the pastor's role to tell the congregant what it means and what parts are important. Such an attitude leaves far too many spiritually impoverished. It wasn't until I began reading the Bible for myself, earnestly and thoroughly, that I began to understand the gospel and God's plans. Multitudes of others have had the same experience.

If you've never approached the Bible in this way, I encourage you to do so with humility and expectation. If your goal is to know whether God has spoken, he will make this clear through the Bible. If you desire to understand what God has said about the things that are of eternal importance, he will reward such a desire. Our surest authority for God's truth is God's Word.

Missing the Mark

Dick Fosbury is a retired Olympic athlete who revolutionized the high jump event. Prior to Fosbury, jumpers leapt over the bar forward, but Fosbury tried something very different: jumping backward over the bar. By arching his back, he slightly shifted the center of gravity to his advantage. The "Fosbury flop" allowed him to jump higher and capture the 1968 gold medal. The current world record of 8 feet and ¼ inch, set by Cuban Javier Sotomayer using the Fosbury flop, has held since 1993. The flop allowed for higher jumps, but what if the rules were such that to qualify for the Olympics, a jumper had to clear 12 feet, or even 10? No one could possibly jump that high, you would say. Everyone would fall short of the mark.

Coming Up Short

We see a similar idea of coming up short when we look at what the Bible says about sin. Paul wrote, "All have sinned and fall short of the glory of God" (Rom. 3:23). The reason we fall short is because the standard is not "better than someone else," but perfection—a perfect man, Jesus Christ. The idea of falling short, of missing the mark, is but one of the ways Scripture speaks of sin. Other words the Bible uses include *iniquity*, *stain*, *trespass*, and *transgression*. The latter two have the idea of overstepping a boundary, of going where one shouldn't. This sort of sin is nearly as old as the world itself.

Adam and Eve overstepped a boundary God had given them. Eat of any tree, except the one in the middle of the garden, he said. When they ate of that tree, they transgressed and came under judgment. The word *stain* highlights the effects of our wrongdoing. It leaves a mark on us, or spiritually speaking, in us. And this is where Adam's sin stains us. We were all "in Adam" when he chose to disobey God, and as his descendants, we inherited his nature. That nature is sinful and fallen, a nature that wants to do evil.

There Are No Good People

We can see how quickly Adam's heirs began to act on this by the description given in Genesis 6, a few chapters after the Garden of Eden. "The Lord saw that the wickedness of man was great in the earth, and that every intention of the thoughts of his heart was only evil continually" (Gen. 6:5). Look at the exclusivity of the language in this verse. Every intention, only evil, continually. Perhaps you doubt that conclusion. You may think that we as people have learned; we have improved; we have overcome our baser urges. Surely, we are not that bad.

The massive Ken Burns documentary film *The Vietnam War* chronicles the Asian conflict that proved to be such a lasting cultural wound to the United States. In episode seven, Captain Matt Harrison reflects on what he saw happening among the men he led.

> One of the things that I learned is that the veneer of civilization is very thin on me, probably on you and I think on everybody. I just saw over and over again some nice young guy out of, say, Huron, South Dakota, who back in Huron helped old ladies across the street and went to church every Sunday. It did not take long for that veneer of civilization to erode. And he was now capable of doing things that just simply are inhuman.[1]

Missing the Mark

It isn't just Captain Harrison's experiences, but Scripture likewise tells us there isn't a distinction. This propensity is within all of us. The evil we see in others is in me and in you. All people are children of Adam, and although the display of sin may vary from person to person, it is false to believe that we are different, that we are better. There are no good people, only people who do a better job of masking it than others. Do you take your place as one who is sinful and rebellious against God? Do you recognize that within your heart you have the same desire for disobedience that Adam and Eve showed when they turned from God?

Some balk at the idea that Adam's sin has tainted them. Let's set aside Adam for a moment. Look at your own heart. This is where we usually begin to compare ourselves with others. We pay our taxes, we do no violence to others, and we give to charity. We are, relatively speaking, pretty good. But comparisons such as this are inaccurate. We can always find someone worse than ourselves, and since we usually choose our best moments to compare to their worst, we're always okay. It is further inaccurate because it is a truncated view of sin. It's not just the acts and deeds we do, but our attitudes and intentions that are sinful.

The apostle Paul has a few "vice lists" in the New Testament, and they include things like malice, gossip, envy, getting angry, ungratefulness, and strife. These are internal heart attitudes. Have you ever considered that such things as these demonstrate your sinful heart? Quite apart from what Adam did, look at your own heart and mind, and can you honestly say you are free from such attitudes? No one can truthfully say so. Our hearts and minds are a petri dish of sin.

It is important to not pass over this too quickly. It is not a matter of "nobody's perfect," or "we all make mistakes." These are the ways we excuse our "shortcomings" or "faults." But a biblical picture of sin is more robust than this and won't allow us to dismiss it with a nod to our human frailty. Author Jerry Bridges writes:

In our human values of civil laws, we draw a huge distinction between an otherwise 'law-abiding citizen' who gets an occasional traffic ticket and a person who lives a 'lawless' life in contempt and utter disregard for all laws. But the Bible doesn't seem to make that distinction. Rather, it simply says sin—that is, all sin without distinction—is lawlessness.[2]

Sin Separates Us from God

Another constant with sin is that it causes separation, not only between people, but also from God, as was the effect in Eden. After they had sinned, Adam and Eve hid themselves from God's presence. The breach caused by sin is still apparent centuries later when the Hebrew prophet Isaiah wrote to Israel:

> Your iniquities have made a separation
> between you and your God,
> and your sins have hidden his face from you
> so that he does not hear.
>
> —Isaiah 59:2

Sin created a division in the relationship between God and his people. It was not he who withdrew from them, but by their sin, they caused a break between themselves and their maker. Cultural faith tends to dismiss this. "Of course human beings are sinful, but God's love overcomes our sin, and its consequences." That explanation is misguided and insufficient. Blogger Tim Challies puts it this way:

> The basic human condition is to believe that God isn't really all that holy and that I'm not really that bad. *God is lenient toward sin, and, as it happens, I am not really all that deeply sinful anyway. So we are a good match, God and I.* It takes no faith to believe that. It takes no great change of mind and heart.[3]

This is another way of saying that we don't really believe our sin has caused a division between God and us. To justify that, we have to use a definition of sin that has two false features. First, it is entirely interpersonal. It only matters how we interact with those around us, and by looking at how we treat others we get a picture of sin. If we are civil and respectful toward them, if we are doing unto others as we would have them do unto us, we are okay. It does not consider how God views our sin and whether it has caused a breach with him. Second, we are again limiting sin to the external. Our attitudes and dispositions aren't sin, only what we openly express and act on. But as we saw earlier, that won't harmonize with what Scripture declares. The Bible goes beyond action in defining sin. It extends to our thoughts and attitudes, even if we never act on them.

If we're to think rightly about sin, we need to recognize the difference between sins and sin. This is the same as the difference between symptoms and a disease. In medicine, there are many ways to control symptoms, sometimes so effectively that a person doesn't even feel sick. But if a doctor did that with a terminal disease, think of the outcome. That would send someone to their death because it is masking the problem, and the same is true with sin. We can be effective at controlling our behavior, and it deludes us into thinking we have conquered sin. But we sin because we are sinners, we act and think because of who we are. Our sin doesn't need symptom management; it needs a cure because it is a terminal disease.

The first step in treatment of a disease is to acknowledge it. No one seeks help for an illness they don't think they have. With many, this is their stance with sin. They believe God has already forgiven them simply because he is loving and merciful. This is like a person who stops his ears at the doctor saying "you have cancer" and instead shouts, "I am well, I am well!" It would be foolish to treat a serious disease like this, to not admit the problem. A faith that does not take

God's declarations about sin seriously is like a patient who refuses to hear a grim diagnosis because they don't want to be upset.

In his letter to the church in Rome, the apostle Paul talks about how sin shows itself. He summarizes the guilt of all mankind to say, "None is righteous, no not one; no one understands; no one seeks for God. All have turned aside; together they have become worthless; no one does good, not even one" (Rom. 3:10–12). That is a comprehensive indictment on all humanity. It includes me; it includes you. There is a cure for sin, to be sure, but if we don't recognize the depth of our alienation from God and how far our sin has separated us from him, we will not seek that cure.

If we doubt that we are really as sinful as Scripture portrays all mankind to be, we will regard what God has done to pardon our sin as something "nice to have" but not entirely necessary. The forgiveness of our sin was costly. It required the death of Jesus Christ, and the outpouring of his blood. Thinking little of sin means we will think little of that sacrifice. The death of Christ is a demonstration of God's love, but it is also a demonstration of his hatred of sin. If our sin were not so bad, it would not have required so great a price as the death of God's only Son.

Guilt as a Spiritual Thermometer

Illness often comes with things like a fever, which is in fact the body's way of trying to deal with disease. Guilt is a kind of spiritual fever that alerts us to a problem. Society has gone to great lengths to excise guilt, to brand it a negative emotion we should not entertain. But guilt is one way God uses to point out our sin. It has value in causing us to understand the separation from God that sin has caused.

In prior ages, most people accepted their guilt before God as legitimate, but they sought to assuage it by doing more, or by doing what the church told them they must do. But the New Testament is clear that no amount of doing can remove our guilt. Only the death of Christ on the cross suffices for that.

The current culture has taken a different approach to guilt. Guilt is seen by many as unhealthy and a barrier to the self-esteem everyone should have. The way to get free of guilt is to understand that it's wrong to experience it, wrong to feel it. When a person does this, it involves denying sin as well. There is no need to feel guilty, because what I've done isn't wrong.

But pretending guilt and sin are not real isn't the way to deal with them, not according to Scripture, that is. God's promise is forgiveness for the one who comes to Jesus in repentance and faith. Trusting him and counting on his promise is but to believe God and to be free of the guilt of sin.

Perhaps you've felt guilt in the past but become good at stifling it, at silencing that voice of conscience that says you are wrong. The sort of guilt that makes you uncomfortable because you know you have fallen short of God's standard is something you shouldn't dismiss. Such guilt is an invitation to think differently about your sin than what the surrounding culture is telling you. I encourage you to consider not what others say about your sin, but what God says about it.

The Love of God

No coin can have a single side. In this chapter and the next, I consider God's love and his justice, two aspects of his character that many have labored to separate or to declare in conflict with one another. But when considered in their full meaning, it is clear that they belong together; indeed, they complement each other and work together to glorify God. The character and attributes of the eternal God are not such that we can explain them without considering the whole of what God tells us in the Bible.

The love of God is an odd juncture where truth and error coalesce, in the minds of people, that is. I call it an odd juncture because those who look to the Scriptures as the basis of truth rightly affirm God's love for sinful humanity. But those who have no particular view of the Bible as the inerrant Word of God also affirm God's love. Yet these two groups are likely to come to different conclusions about what God's love means, why he has expressed his love for us, and the extent of his love.

God Loves the World

Without question, the most famous verse in the Bible is John 3:16: "For God so loved the world, that he gave his only Son, that whoever believes in him should not perish but have eternal life." Too frequently we pass over the tremendous truth this verse contains!

Note that God is the source of this love. It is he who has loved the world, a world that, recalling Genesis 6, had become only evil continually. God had created the world and mankind very good, but sin came in to mar and degrade that creation—including mankind—and to make it very bad.

The cultural believer is apt to think that God loves her because she is lovable. She is basically a good person, and not that bad; therefore, it makes sense that God loves her. D.A. Carson summarizes this: "Nowadays if you tell people that God loves them, they are unlikely to be surprised. Of course God loves me; he's like that, isn't he? Besides, why shouldn't he love me? I'm kind of cute, or at least as nice as the next person. I'm okay, you're okay, and God loves you and me."[1]

The Bible declares God's love for his creation, and for sinners, but it makes clear that God loves us not because of who we are, but *in spite of* who we are. The apostle Paul puts it this way: "God shows his love for us in that while we were still sinners, Christ died for us" (Rom. 5:8). The phrase *while we were sinners* reminds us that in ourselves we aren't all around lovable. We are God's enemies. This is a part of God's love that makes it so astounding. It is not out of obligation or compulsion that God loves us and gave his Son for us. Rather, it is his great mercy and kindness that expresses his love through the giving of his Son.

Moreover, the love of God is an active love. He gave his Son as the sacrifice for our sins. The Lord Jesus also died for sinful humanity willingly. Speaking of his life, he told his disciples, "No one takes it from me, but I lay it down of my own accord" (John 10:18). The love of God seeks out sinners who are in no way seeking him. As sinful men and women who would prefer to go our own way, to be our own masters, God's love reaches out to us and offers us not an insurance policy against future judgment, but a present and ongoing relationship with the creator of all things.

God's love is also an overcoming love. Years ago, our family visited Meramec Caverns in Missouri, an underground series of caves that are remarkable for the formations and architecture shaped only by flowing water. One of the things the guide does is to extinguish all the lights, to show what true darkness is. This is difficult to experience above ground because there is always some ambient light that makes total darkness very rare. After a moment, the guide will strike a single match, and there is a blaze of light filling the cavern. That single match seems very bright because of the enveloping darkness around it.

This illustrates God's love. Not that it is small like a single match, but that we need to understand the surrounding darkness to truly appreciate it. We need to see that God's love entered a world that was opposed to him—that remains opposed to him—and gave his Son to die for his rebellious creatures. God's love is remarkable for what it overcomes.

The barrier to fellowship and intimacy with God is our sin. Though we may not think so, we are opposed to God in heart and mind. Our hearts want what makes us comfortable and what pleases us. That comfort can be both physical and spiritual, and these desires work themselves out in self-serving ways that move us far from God. If we fail to see the darkness of our sin, we dismiss the fact that the light of God's love overcomes that darkness. We don't believe there is anything to overcome.

If God Loves the World, Won't All Be Saved?

It's a common belief that since God's love is so great, so expansive, that this means all will be saved. What accompanies this belief is that putting one's trust in the Lord Jesus isn't necessary. As I've seen on a bumper sticker, "God bless the whole world, no exceptions." God's blessing does indeed extend to all. As Jesus said, God "makes his sun rise on the evil and on the good, and sends rain on the just and on the unjust" (Matt. 5:45). But that is not the same as saying everyone is redeemed, everyone is forgiven, everyone will spend eternity in heaven. John 3:16, again, says that God loved the world. In short, there is no one who is not the object of that love. But it also says that in his love he gave his Son. The guilt of our sin required the payment for it, but the love of God alone is not the basis of forgiveness. In addition to his gospel, John later wrote several letters of the New Testament, and near the end of his first letter he writes this: "This is love: not that we loved God, but that he loved us and sent his Son as an atoning sacrifice for our sins" (1 John 4:10 NIV).

The atoning sacrifice of the Lord Jesus on the cross is the basis of our forgiveness, and the cross encompasses the two truths that God is love and that God is just. If we disregard the cross as the expression of God's wrath against sin, we also end up with a skewed understanding of God's love. He loves us to such an extent that he would even send his own Son to absorb the punishment for our sin.

Does it have to be so? Why can't God simply apply the death of Christ to all, regardless of their unbelief? The gospel is an invitation to come to the one who can pardon us of our sins and remove our guilt. There is no shortage of questions we can ask about why God has ordered his universe as he has, why he has planned salvation as he has. They are not all answered for us, but the ones that are give us all we need to understand the love of God in the offer of salvation. We focus too much on the "why can't God" instead of the "why has God" questions. Why has God loved the world enough to send his only Son to die for us? We who wanted nothing to do with him, who set ourselves against him—this is the world that John 3 says God has so loved!

John 3:16 also says that "whoever believes" should not perish. The death of Christ and the forgiveness it brings is not mine or yours by default. We must take hold of it by faith. If someone wins the lottery, the state doesn't send them a check. The winner must claim the prize. If they don't do so, they don't receive the money. Similarly, the New Testament repeatedly urges those who hear the message to believe in the Lord Jesus.

The cultural Christian is apt to think that those who take the Scriptures seriously are downplaying God's love, not appreciating it, because they keep talking about sin. In fact, it is only those who are born again that comprehend that love. John again marvels to exclaim, "See how much the Father has loved us! His love is so great that we are called God's children—and so, in fact, we are" (1 John 3:1 GNT).

In the book of Revelation, John writes, "To him who loves us and has freed us from our sins by his blood . . . to him be glory and dominion forever and ever. Amen" (Rev. 1:5–6). In other words, God not only loves us, but frees us from our sins, and this is by the blood of Jesus. This freedom is available to all, but only those who have been born again experience it.

The proof and demonstration of God's love, says John, is the cross. The death of Christ on the cross is a proclamation that the God of the universe loves his creatures and has made a way for them to be reconciled to him. When we meditate on the cross, and on the death of Jesus, we begin to understand just how much God loves us. But we also see the punishment for our sin, poured out on another. We see God exercising both love and justice.

It is a hallmark of cultural Christianity to emphasize God's love to the near exclusion of all other attributes, but Scripture presents a more comprehensive portrait of the character and nature of God. Understanding that full picture to include wrath against sin as well as his love for sinners is vital to getting a true view of him.

The Wrath of God

God's wrath is an uncomfortable topic for many people. We don't like to think of God as angry with us or anyone. In the shifting ground of public opinion, the idea of God's wrath seems downright intolerant. Western society has taken pains to rid itself of these ideas, and that includes those who claim a relationship with God. Some point to passages of Scripture that seem to dispense with his wrath, such as "God is love" (1 John 4:8), or "love covers a multitude of sins" (1 Pet. 4:8). The truth of these verses, like anything else we know about God's attributes, must be compared and harmonized with the whole of Scripture. As John Blanchard says, "Although 'God is love' is the truth, it is not the only truth."[1]

Many people fail on this point, discharging parts of the Bible with a "that was then, this is now" attitude. It's common for many to think of God revealed in the Old Testament as vengeful and angry, while only in the New Testament is the love of God made known.

Is the God of the Old Testament Different?

The Old Testament does not present a monolithic portrait of God. God's love is clearly displayed to Israel, his chosen people. He loved them and redeemed them from slavery. Why did he do this? Deuteronomy 7 comes closest to giving an answer. "It was not because you were more in number than any other people that the

LORD set his love on you and chose you, for you were the fewest of all peoples, but it is because the LORD loves you and is keeping the oath that he swore to your fathers" (Deut. 7:7–8). In short, God loved them because he loved them!

Recognizing that the Bible tells one story, it is erroneous to try to divide God's character in this way, saying he was one thing in the Old Testament and a different thing in the New. When we come to the New Testament, Jesus himself spoke much about hell and judgment. Matthew 11:20–23 is but one passage that records this:

> Then he began to denounce the cities where most of his mighty works had been done, because they did not repent. "Woe to you, Chorazin! Woe to you, Bethsaida! For if the mighty works done in you had been done in Tyre and Sidon, they would have repented long ago in sackcloth and ashes. But I tell you, it will be more bearable on the day of judgment for Tyre and Sidon than for you. And you, Capernaum, will you be exalted to heaven? You will be brought down to Hades."

There is clearly wrath and judgment coming to the inhabitants of these cities.

In the final book of the New Testament, Revelation, there is also much about wrath and judgment. The book depicts Jesus himself as judge.

> From his mouth comes a sharp sword with which to strike down the nations, and he will rule them with a rod of iron. He will tread the winepress of the fury of the wrath of God the Almighty. On his robe and on his thigh he has a name written, King of kings and Lord of lords (Rev. 19:15–16).

All Scripture, then, teaches the wrath of God, and we must account for it in our understanding of God and his character. We shouldn't soft-pedal this aspect of God's revelation because it is painful or distasteful to us. The question, rather, is why does God have wrath or anger? The answer is sin. Psalm 5:5–6 is one example of God's posture toward sin and—since mankind sins—toward sinners: "The boastful shall not stand before your eyes; you hate all evildoers. You destroy those who speak lies; the LORD abhors the bloodthirsty and deceitful man."

A few chapters on, in Psalm 11:5, we read also, "His soul hates the wicked and the one who loves violence." Recall again that the definition of evil that is significant is not ours, but God's. It is not important whether we think of ourselves as sinful, but whether God does.

God Shouldn't Be Angry

In their own understanding, some think that God should set aside his anger and simply overlook sin. If he were only to do so, there is no need for him to be angry. After all, we are only human, and surely God knows and understands our weaknesses, doesn't he? He understands our propensity to turn from him and in his kindness, love must be the highest of his attributes. This thinking is attractive, and it sounds logical to many. But it, too, is flawed because it does not consider that God's wrath conforms to his justice.

The justice of God is an attribute that many want to invoke as a comfort when a horrible wrong occurs. We've all heard or read the phrase, "There's a special place in hell for such people." This thinking reckons that God will be just and not allow an evil person to get away with their crime. The outrage we feel at the abuse of children, or at other horrific crimes, demonstrates that we agree it is just for God to be angry at such people. But we are slower to apply that wrath to ourselves. The justice of God means that he punishes sin, and that justice does not grade on a curve. All sin and all sinners are under the wrath of God. Our failure to see this is not because God has changed, but because our attitudes have.

Jonathan Edwards is perhaps the most famous preacher of early American history. His best-known sermon is titled "Sinners in the Hands of an Angry God." Edwards was no firebrand preacher who shouted and railed at his audience. In fact, one can scarcely say he preached this sermon. Rather, he read his words from his manuscript. What made it so famous was the response from the congregation. Edward's hearers trembled, wailed audibly, and grabbed on to the pews for fear that God would open the floor to swallow them up right then.

We are apt to dismiss this reaction with bemused wonder at the naïveté of an eighteenth-century audience. But were Edward's hearers mistaken about God's wrath? Were they incorrect that God is angry at sin, and that the Bible promises retribution for sin? The brief survey of passages we've looked at, and indeed the whole tenor of Scripture, testifies that God's wrath toward sinners is another truth in Scripture that's hard to mistake. A.W. Tozer put it this way:

> God's justice stands forever against the sinner in utter severity. The vague and tenuous hope that God is too kind to punish the ungodly has become a deadly opiate for the consciences of millions. It hushes their fears and allows them to practice all pleasant forms of iniquity while death draws every day nearer and the command to repent goes unregarded.[2]

No doubt, many have convinced themselves of this, that God is unconcerned about sin, that anger and wrath are unbecoming of a loving God. If this describes you, if you have counted on the love of God alone to overcome all your rebellion toward him, I urge you to look at the message God has given. You count on his promises of love and forgiveness, as well you should. But he also made promises of judgment upon sinners. It is self-delusion to reckon upon the one but discount the other. We cannot divide God in such a fashion as to say we believe him implicitly when he promises his love toward us, but we reject as offensive any promises he has made about his wrath against sin.

"I Don't Think a Loving God Would Do That."

Part of our confusion on this stems from our incorrect assumptions about God's thoughts and about our position. "I don't think a loving God would send people to hell." That's a common idea, but behind it are a few flawed beliefs. First, it is clearly not informed by the Bible, but rather by human sentimentality. It fashions the sovereign God to be a monochromatic deity whose highest purpose is the personal comfort of his creatures. The Bible presents God as merciful *and* just, as gracious *and* righteous. We do not arrive at a truer picture of God by saying one of these attributes abolishes all others. Even in human relationships, we can see the false logic of this. Pastor Timothy Keller, who hears this reasoning often, writes:

> I always start my response by pointing out that all loving persons are sometimes filled with wrath, not just despite of but because of their love. If you love a person and you see someone ruining them—even they themselves—you get angry.... The Bible says that God's wrath flows from his love and delight in his creation. He is angry at evil and injustice because it is destroying its peace and integrity.[3]

When the prophet Isaiah saw a vision of God seated on his heavenly throne, one of the angels said:

> "Holy, holy, holy is the LORD of hosts;
> the whole earth is full of his glory!"
>
> —Isaiah 6:3

Holiness, then, is an integral part of God's character and identity that is woven seamlessly together with his justice. Isaiah's response to this vision is important, too. "Woe is me! For I am lost; for I am a man of unclean lips, and I dwell in the midst of a people of unclean lips" (Isa. 6:5). Isaiah didn't just point a finger at someone else. He acknowledged his own sin and the justice of God. When we understand God's holiness, one of the first things we do is acknowledge our own sin and guilt. If this has never been your experience, perhaps it means you don't have an accurate picture of God and his character.

God's hatred of sin flows from his holiness, and his exercise of judgment for sin is a result of that justice. If we want to see justice done on the earth, to see justice done in human affairs, part of that is the confidence that a just God reigns.

Thinking it wrong of God to be angry also assumes that mankind's default position is one of goodness, and it is only because God came along and spoiled it all that some are judged anyway. But goodness is not our natural state, or normal condition; evil and rebellion against God are. What if we turned the previous statement around? "I don't think a just God would send evil people to heaven." This gets at the other side of the truth about mankind. We were not just fine, ambling our way to heaven, until God came along to throw a penalty flag, as it were, and threaten us with judgment. Rather, we are on a path to destruction, and the wonder of the gospel is that God provides a way of deliverance from the well-deserved judgment due to us!

This is an area where God's truth has been turned upside down by so many for so long that when people encounter what the Bible really says it seems incredible. It doesn't take some great failure or moral lapse to deserve hell. It is the natural disposition of our hearts to be in rebellion against God. On the contrary, we are naturally fit for hell, but only supernaturally fit for heaven.

One can see this as a kind of "leading spiritual indicator." That is, if someone protests that they aren't as bad as some other people,

The Wrath of God

that they do their best, that they surely have some qualities of character that God would commend—this is an indication that a person doesn't really understand what God says about the sinful state of every human heart. On the other side, a believer quite freely acknowledges that they are every bit as sinful as the Bible describes. They rejoice, not because they are sinful, but because God saves such sinners who humble themselves before him.

Admitting these truths about ourselves goes a long way to resolving our discomfort about God's wrath. When I consider that I deserve God's wrath, I take his side in the matter. I silence that little lawyer within myself who wants to say "I object!" to God's assessment of me. I instead acknowledge that God's wrath is real and merited, yet that is not the sum of the story. God poured out the wrath that I deserved onto the Lord Jesus. God's wrath was not turned aside by his love; rather, his love provided the One who bore that wrath.

The reality of God's wrath does not mean that it must inevitably fall on us. It will fall on those who do not turn to Christ. Deliverance from God's wrath, from the punishment for our sins, is the promise of the gospel. Indeed, even in the Old Testament God had made this clear. "As I live, declares the Lord God, I have no pleasure in the death of the wicked, but that the wicked turn from his way and live; turn back, turn back from your evil ways, for why will you die, O house of Israel?" (Eze. 33:11). The prophet did nothing but call the people to admit their condition and turn from it, and to turn toward God. That turning is called repentance.

Turning from Sin

What, then, will you do with these truths? God is love, and the giving of his Son shows that. But God is also just and holy, and he will judge sin. The death of Jesus shows that as well. The response the Bible calls people to is known as repentance. We need to look a bit at what repentance is not to better understand what it is.

Dental Chair Repentance
When I was a kid, I had great and serious dealings with God about every six months or so. These interactions coincided with my semiannual visits to the dentist. Like many, I hated the dentist and dreaded any time I had an appointment. Too often, as well, I had a cavity, and so would follow the novocaine and the drilling. Oh, the drilling! This would precipitate earnest prayer on my part. These were the sorts of prayers where I would cry out for help, for relief. I just hated the whole experience, the pain, the smell of it all. So, I would beg and plead for relief, asking God for mercy. If he would show me mercy, I resolved to be a better person, to focus more on God and to live rightly. I can't exactly recall the specifics of what, in my adolescent mind, focusing more on God would mean, but that was my resolution. This may have been a cry for help, but it wasn't repentance. It wasn't informed by what Scripture said. I wasn't really thinking about the offense of my sin.

I would later dub this exercise "dental chair repentance." There are variations on this theme, the spare-tire concept of God, for example. It means crying out to God only when one is in difficulty, or when one's comfort or peace is threatened. Without question, the Bible is full of examples of asking God for help. King David, in the book of Psalms, cries out for deliverance from his enemies. They were pursuing him, seeking to take his life, and David prayed, "Be pleased, O LORD, to deliver me! O LORD, make haste to help me!" (Ps. 40:13).

The difference with David is that he had a relationship with God. He knew God, he followed God—David was, as the prophet Samuel said, "a man after [God's] own heart" (1 Sam. 13:14). When David pleaded with God for help, he was not a stranger to God, nor God to him. From his youth, he had meditated on God and on who he is. Facing Goliath, an opponent that King Saul doubted David would stand a chance against, David answered, "The LORD who delivered me from the paw of the lion and from the paw of the bear will deliver me from the hand of this Philistine" (1 Sam. 17:37). I have faced formidable opponents before, David said, and God delivered me. I know him and his character, and I trust him. The other difference is that the motivation for dental chair repentance is not that I have understood my failure and my sin. Rather, it is that I am in trouble, and I want to get out of it!

Many people want this sort of help when they face a huge challenge in their life. They want God to deliver them and save them. But unlike David, they don't have a relationship with God. They know God as they know the plumber. The sink is backed up and so they call someone to fix it. And fix it he does, but do they call the plumber the next day, just to talk? Do they ask the plumber about his thoughts, his desires? They wouldn't do this because they don't have a relationship with the plumber.

The relationship this describes is one that's devoid of repentance; that is, it lacks a change of mind and heart. When the New Testament

Turning from Sin

speaks about repentance, this begins with a change of mind, a turning around. Imagine someone traveling a country road, and they come to a place where the road is barricaded. A large sign reads, "Bridge out 1 mile." The driver slows as she approaches, does a three-point turn, and goes back in the direction she came. Another driver comes along, stops his car, and gets out. He removes the barricade, dragging it out of the road. He gets back in his car and drives on in the direction of the missing bridge. Which of these two repented? Obviously, the first driver turned around and went the opposite direction of the danger. The second did not. That person did not turn, did not repent.

The Bible is full of such road signs. They warn us of the dangers of sin and of the peril of continuing ahead on a path where the bridge is out. The apostle Peter, when preaching to his fellow Jews who had so recently rejected their Messiah in favor of a criminal, said to them, "Repent therefore, and turn back, that your sins may be blotted out" (Acts 3:19). Part of Peter's call is for the people to admit their error in not believing in the one God had sent, to change their minds about God's Son. In fact, just prior to this, Peter had said to them, "Brothers, I know that you acted in ignorance, as did also your rulers. But what God foretold by the mouth of all the prophets, that his Christ would suffer, he thus fulfilled" (Acts 3:17–18). In other words, they acted ignorantly in their rejection of the Lord Jesus. They could not make such a claim now. Peter had told them plainly of their offense against God and who Jesus was.

The call was to change their minds and to act on that change of mind. That is, turn back from your previous unbelief about the Lord and believe who the Scriptures proclaim him to be. It is important to see that this change of mind is not plucking up one's courage or resolving to do better. These are self-centered activities that might make us feel good inwardly, but they don't really address our true need. Repentance is a two-way kind of activity. We turn from sin and toward God. It is taking the facts of the Bible about the person of the

Lord Jesus as true, and if true, these facts demand a decision. Harry Ironside, a preacher of the mid-twentieth century, put it this way:

> To hear the Word is to receive God's testimony, and that is the very essence of repentance. When he who has spurned that Word bows to its message, even though it tells him he is lost and undone and has no righteousness of his own, he turns from his vain thoughts and accepts instead the testimony of the Lord. It is to such a one that the Holy Spirit delights to present a crucified, risen, and exalted Christ as the one supreme object of faith.[1]

Ironside notes that the crux of repentance is to agree with God. We agree with him not only that our sin is as bad as God says it is, but that sin has separated us from him. For many, this remains a huge hurdle in apprehending spiritual truth. They really don't accept that they are sinful, or if they are, it's not all that bad. And we are all experts at self-justification, and of rationalizing our behavior. We have good reasons for the decisions we've made, and even if what we did was wrong, we are sure that God understands we're only human! Indeed, we are only human, but to be human is to be a sinner, and to be as great a sinner as Scripture says we are. The first step of repentance is to come over to God's viewpoint on this most important fact.

Repentance as a Heart Habit

If repentance is a first step in coming to salvation, it does not mean that we leave it behind once we are born again. We have an ongoing need for repentance throughout all life. Martin Luther launched the Reformation of the church by nailing the 95 Theses, or points for debate, to the church door in Wittenberg. The first of them said this: "When our Lord and Master Jesus Christ said, 'Repent,' he willed the entire life of believers to be one of repentance."

Turning from Sin

It is not just at the beginning, but throughout the whole of life that believers must practice repentance. It is but another way of describing a disciple, one who follows. If the path goes left, we turn, if the path goes right, we turn.

I spent the early part of my professional life as a musician in a symphony orchestra. One of the things that a musician must develop is their ear—that is, to be able to discern when you are playing out of tune or when you are out of rhythm. Playing a stringed instrument is different from playing the piano, where when you strike the key, there is no changing the pitch. But as a string player, you learn to hear fine gradations in the pitch so that you know whether the note is too high, too low, or correct.

This is similar to repentance. Christians learn when they are "out of tune" with God and they adjust—at least they should. They learn when their "rhythm" with God is off. In fact, the apostle Paul says something quite close to this when he urges the Christians in the region of Galatia, "Let us also keep in step with the Spirit" (Gal. 5:25).

Some of my colleagues were fond of saying that string playing is rapid adjustment. No one plays in tune all the time. The question is, do you quickly adjust to get back in tune? Trevin Wax describes the practice of repentance the following way and notes the difference between a believer and one who is not:

> The difference between a Christian and a non-Christian is not that the non-Christian sins and the Christian does not, but that the Christian sins *and repents*, while the unbeliever hardens their heart toward God—either by refusing to admit the sin or by trying to deal with the sin in some other way.[2]

Imagine a musician clearly out of tune who insists it must be the others who are playing wrong notes. If you've never thought that you have any need for repentance, perhaps it's because you're not considering that you're out of step with God's Spirit, that you're not walking rightly.

Paul wrote to the Christians in Rome that believers in Jesus should not have a static relationship with him, but "be transformed by the renewal of your mind, that by testing you may discern what is the will of God" (Rom. 12:2). Here again is the transformative nature of a relationship with Jesus, and where it comes together with repentance is in the renewal of the mind. Our thoughts about God, sin, ourselves—these things begin to change once we are born again, and they continue to change along the path of discipleship.

In the letter to the Ephesians, Paul wrote, "You must no longer walk as the Gentiles do, in the futility of their minds" (Eph. 4:17). Gentiles were the unbelievers all around the earliest Christians. They were going in a different direction from the Christians, and indeed some of the Christians had once been among them. Paul tells them, "But that is not the way you learned Christ!" (Eph. 4:20). Learning Christ is in one sense to learn to be counter-cultural. The world that does not submit to Jesus Christ is always a culture against him. Christians are continually repenting and continually seeking to conform their lives to him, and not to the surrounding culture. This is yet another way of describing the ongoing repentance that should characterize Christians. If this seems foreign to you, it likely indicates a cultural faith that isn't taking God's viewpoint, isn't agreeing with God that we all need repentance.

Turning to God

In the book of Acts, we read about Paul and his fellow gospel worker Silas being arrested in the city of Philippi in Asia Minor. They are miraculously freed as the doors of the jail swing open. The jailer is full of fear when he sees all this, and running into Paul and Silas, he asks, "What must I do to be saved?" (Acts 16:30). Their answer is simple and brief: "Believe in the Lord Jesus, and you will be saved" (Acts 16:31). There is more to what they said than this, as Luke, the writer of Acts tells us. "And they spoke the word of the Lord to him and to all who were in his house" (Acts 16:32). In other words, they preached the gospel to this man, and to others in his house, and explained to him who Jesus is and what he has done in his death and resurrection. While the gospel can be explained briefly, that doesn't mean it's without deeper significance or meaning. The only way to learn these things is to look at Scripture.

Seeing Jesus as Scripture Presents Him

To believe in Jesus, we must know something about him, the facts about who he is and what he has done. Throughout the book of Acts, we find the apostles explaining these facts about Jesus, of sin and repentance. What they preached in Acts is introduced in the Gospels, and by looking there, we learn a few foundational things.

At the start of the Gospel of Matthew, the announcement came to Joseph that Mary would have a son. The angelic instruction was, "You shall call his name Jesus, for he will save his people from their sins" (Matt. 1:21). The name *Jesus* means "God saves." There is thus a direct connection between the name of Jesus and salvation. This is important because for many, Jesus is a great teacher, a peerless example, or one who taught humanity the right way to live. But none of these include Jesus as savior. The second half of the verse demonstrates why we need a savior: our sins. An example or a teacher cannot remove the guilt of our sin, cannot reconcile us to God, and this is why Jesus came to earth.

A few verses later in Matthew 1:23, we find another name for Jesus: "Behold, the virgin shall conceive and bear a son, and they shall call his name Immanuel (which means, God with us)." Matthew interprets the name for us, which speaks to the other side of Jesus's identity, as God incarnate. That is, God taking on humanity. Only God can save, and as both God and man, Jesus is uniquely qualified to be the savior of the world.

Is it necessary to believe these things about Jesus, that he is both God and man, to have a saving relationship with him? Some would say no, it's not critical to believe all those things about Jesus. The important thing is what he taught us, the love he demonstrated. When we follow his example, keeping the Golden Rule, this is what God wants from us.

Jesus surely was a great teacher and he was a selfless practitioner of the Golden Rule, but he is more than that. If Jesus was only a great teacher, it doesn't explain the necessity of his death on the cross. Some regard his death as a great mistake, a profound misunderstanding on the part of both the Roman and Jewish authorities. But Scripture presents the death of Jesus differently. Those who betrayed Jesus and killed him certainly bear responsibility, but it was also part of God's plan that Jesus die. Indeed, this is the reason he came to earth. No one verse of Scripture summarizes these two truths better than Acts 2:23. The apostle Peter, preaching to a crowd, says, "This Jesus, delivered up according to the definite plan and foreknowledge of God, you crucified and killed by the hands of lawless men."

It was God's definite plan to send his Son into the world to die for our sins. It was not a plan B; it was not a surprise to God. God's purpose in redeeming sinners provided that his Son die in their place. This is the heart of the gospel and of salvation. But the second half of the verse makes clear that although God planned to send his Son into the world, mankind bears responsibility for their sin. Lawless men killed the Son of God. Judas, who betrayed the Lord Jesus, is called the son of perdition, or of destruction. Judas was responsible for his own choice to betray God's Son.

So, as to whether it is necessary to believe these things about Jesus, the answer is yes. We must embrace the portrait of the Lord Jesus Christ that Scripture presents, else we risk fashioning a god in our image rather than accepting his self-revelation. I want to again note, I'm not trying to demonstrate to someone who is unfamiliar with the Scriptures or with Jesus who he is. Rather, I am speaking to those who are acquainted with the Bible and who do know the name of Jesus. A disconnect comes if we regard him only as an example to follow. Extolling his example does not bring pardon for sin. The portrait in Scripture is not of Jesus as a good man, a superior example we should follow. The portrait is of one who is the Son of God, divine and eternal, but who came to earth and took on human flesh. He lived a sinless life, died for sinful humanity, and rose again. All these aspects of who Jesus is are vitally important to his identity as savior.

The Good and the Bad
"I'm just hoping that when I get to the end of life, I'll have done more good things than bad." Have you ever heard someone express

this, or a similar thought? It's very common that people think that at the end of their lives, they will approach some grand, heavenly scale. On one side will be all the good things they have done throughout their lives. On the other side, the bad things are placed. If the good outweigh the bad, you get into heaven. There are some variations on this, but this captures the essence of a very human-centered faith, if it can even be called faith.

There are two barriers to this idea. The first is that it depends entirely on what a person does. It is focused on being a "good person," but the definition of a good person is very subjective. Who says what a good person is? It usually means a standard that seems reasonable, fair, and compares people against one another. (To have a good person, one must also have a bad person to set against the good.) But it doesn't include perfection, and that means it is a standard God would not recognize. The apostle Paul speaks of a "day when, according to my gospel, God judges the secrets of men by Christ Jesus" (Rom. 2:16). The standard won't be what we think is good, but a perfect man who never sinned. No one, of course, will measure up.

The second problem is that because this idea is focused on what a person does, it neglects what Jesus has done. His death on the cross is a forceful proclamation that "doing one's best" is not good enough, not by a long shot. No one can work her way into God's family or to heaven. To pursue such a path is to set aside all that God has done in giving his Son to pay for our sins. Ask yourself whether God would give his only Son to die in your place, only to have you say, "Thanks, but I think what I've done is good enough, don't you?"

As common as it is to think in this good versus bad mentality, I urge anyone to search the New Testament for any suggestion that one becomes a Christian by being good or living a good life. You will find nothing of the kind in its pages. Do not confuse this with the commands given to disciples to live in a way that pleases God and honors him. Those commands are indeed important, but they are only applicable to those who are already born again. They have to do with being a follower of Jesus, not becoming one.

We often have a lot to unlearn about what it means to be saved. For many people, this comparison of good and bad is one of the chief things. This is why I keep coming back to the topic of sin and of our inability to overcome it by what we do. The opposite idea is ingrained in us by our peers and by society from an early age. We must be "good" if God is going to let us into heaven, must we not? Thinking in these terms obscures our true need; it clouds our minds into thinking that we really aren't so bad, and so we don't need to be saved because we're not truly lost.

Think for a moment about the word *saved*. The New Testament presents this as a necessity for anyone who would gain eternal life. In an age of acceptance, however, many deny the need to be saved. "Why would I need to be saved, when I've never been lost?" Many of the things we believe both about humanity and God combine to form our views about this. If I believe that mankind is essentially good, then I'm likely to believe that we all start out on the right track. Unless someone does something really evil, there's no reason to think everyone won't one day be with God in heaven.

As attractive as it sounds, it cannot be reconciled with the teaching of Scripture. We don't start out on the right track; we start out as alienated and separated from God. It doesn't take some great moral failure for us to leave the road to heaven. On the contrary, it takes something to get on that road in the first place. The apostle Paul tells the Ephesian Christians that at one time they were "dead in [their] trespasses" (Eph. 2:5). To be dead in sin is the opposite of being in good standing with God. What Paul describes is true of every single one of us. We are not naturally right with God.

I recall hearing a story years ago about a couple of congregants in a local church. The congregation sang the very popular "Amazing Grace" by John Newton.

> Amazing grace! How sweet the sound
> That saved a wretch like me!
> I once was lost, but now am found;
> Was blind but now I see.

At the end of the hymn, one fellow turned to the other and asked, "So, how did God save your wretched soul?" The man replied with indignation, "I beg your pardon!" "But, you just sang it!" replied the questioner.

Are we like that? We sing that God saved our wretched souls, but we really don't believe we're wretched or that we really do need to be saved. We don't believe, as John Newton did, that we are lost. If you've never considered the question of whether you're saved, perhaps it's because you've never considered you're lost.

Crossing Over from Death to Life

The metaphor of birth is frequent in the New Testament because what happens when we trust in the Lord Jesus is we are spiritually reborn. But there are other pictures, too. Crossing over from one condition to another also symbolizes salvation. After telling his hearers that he has all authority to judge, Jesus says this: "I say to you, whoever hears my word and believes him who sent me has eternal life. He does not come into judgment, but has passed from death to life" (John 5:24).

This is why a believer can have confidence that they will not come under judgment for their sins. It is not because they are behaving well, or living a good life, or any other thing religion tells us is necessary. What is of first importance is to believe the testimony of God's Son.

Turning to God

When the nation of Israel came out of Egypt, they were delivered from slavery. God delivered them in a dramatic way, by bringing them through the Red Sea on dry ground. They crossed over from one shore to the other. The Egyptians who followed them were swallowed up in the sea. Israel need never go back to Egypt because God had accomplished their freedom. Many have seen this as a picture of Christian salvation. The New Testament depicts the unsaved person as being enslaved to sin. When we trust in Jesus, we cross over to the other shore. We are delivered not just from the eternal punishment for our sin but from the bondage of sin while we live.

It isn't necessary to be able to say that on a certain day you trusted in the Lord Jesus. For that, too, could become a snare, looking back to the day and the hour, rather than to Jesus himself as the source of your confidence. But you can ask yourself whether you are trusting in the Lord now. You can ask yourself if you've now turned from your sin and your practical disregard of him and have embraced him as the savior. You can ask yourself if you now believe in the one the Scriptures present as the only way to God.

Whatever history you have with the Christian faith, with going to church, or whatever confidence you may have in yourself, none of these are what brings you from death to life. Only the Lord Jesus Christ—faith in him—can do this. The gospel message is simple, but it is not simplistic. The wrath of a holy God was satisfied by the sacrifice of his Son on the cross. God demonstrated that he was satisfied with all that Jesus did, all that he suffered, by raising him from the dead. God calls on all to turn from sin and self and to trust Jesus as the only acceptable substitute. Trusting in him, crossing from death to life, is but the beginning. Jesus also invites us to follow him as disciples.

Follow Me

When Jesus began his public ministry and gathered the twelve disciples around him, his call was simple: follow me. It was not, "Attend church, be good, do your best." None of the things that are often part of cultural Christianity make up the call to discipleship. Rather, discipleship is centered in the person of the Lord Jesus Christ. What things, then, characterize disciples of Jesus? What should it look like to follow him?

Disciples Take Their Identity from Christ
The New Testament presents a picture of mankind as under one of two heads. We are either in Adam, or we are in Christ. To be in Adam, we need do nothing, for we are born into Adam. To be in Christ, we must be born again. The things that characterize those in Adam are sin, spiritual death, separation from God, and condemnation. The things that characterize Christians are forgiveness, life, fellowship with God, and the security of knowing the creator of all things.

How much that little preposition *in* conveys! Paul says that, "In him we have redemption through his blood, the forgiveness of our trespasses, according to the riches of his grace" (Eph. 1:7). The Christian's point of reference is no longer what we were, no longer the world around us. It is now Christ and all that is in him. In the book of Colossians, Paul writes that "in him all things hold together" and that "in him all the fullness of God was pleased to dwell" (Col. 1:17, 19). Everything in the created world relies on Jesus Christ, and he is the full expression of God. The identity of his followers relies on him as well.

Later in this letter, Paul tells them, "For you have died, and your life is hidden with Christ in God. When Christ who is your life appears, then you also will appear with him in glory" (Col. 3:3–4). Believers are so closely linked with the Lord Jesus that when he died, we died in him. This is part of our new identity. The "old me" associated with Adam is now defeated. I do not have to obey the sinful urges that come with everything I was in Adam. As long as we are in these bodies, we struggle to be fully free of those desires. Paul acknowledges this: "Not that I have already obtained this or am already perfect, but I press on to make it my own, because Christ Jesus has made me his own" (Phil. 3:12). He has not achieved full maturity in Christ, but he also knows that what ultimately shapes his identity is that Christ has made him his own.

Disciples Want to Know Him Better through His Word

Followers of Jesus are those who regularly listen to God through his Word. They read the Scriptures, study them, and look to the Bible as the authority for their lives. This does not mean they have no questions about Scripture, face no confusion, or that everything in the Bible is immediately clear to them. It does mean they are seeking to know God better through his Word, and they continue in that desire. When he was soon to ascend to heaven, Jesus met two disciples on the road to Emmaus. The disciples do not immediately recognize Jesus, and after questioning them about what happened recently in Jerusalem, he says to them, "'O foolish ones, and slow of heart to believe all that the prophets have spoken! Was it not necessary that the Christ should suffer these things and enter into his glory?' And beginning with Moses and all the Prophets, he interpreted to them in all the Scriptures the things concerning himself" (Luke 24:25–27).

This demonstrates that from Genesis through to Malachi, the last book of the Old Testament, there are truths about the Lord Jesus. He is the subject of prophecy and prediction. At the time, this was the only Bible his followers had; the New Testament was not yet written. The Old Testament is not just a Jewish history book. Rather, it is the record of God's promised Messiah and the revealing of God's glory through the plan of salvation.

The way of growth and discipleship is through engagement with the Bible. Increasing in the knowledge of God and his character, knowing who he really is, is not possible if we don't read the Bible. Rituals or rites celebrated in a church service are not the way. The New Testament never teaches this. The apostles instead point to God's truth, through his Word, as the way we grow. Peter ascribes new life in Christ to the Word of God and the message it brings. "You have been born again, not of perishable seed but of imperishable, through the living and abiding word of God" (1 Peter 1:23). Paul tells the Ephesians that it is part of their defense against the devil, calling them to "take the helmet of salvation, and the sword of the Spirit, which is the word of God" (Eph. 6:17). To use a sword effectively, one needs to know how to wield it, and that comes through practice, through familiarity. Writing to Timothy, Paul reminds him "from childhood you have been acquainted with the sacred writings, which are able to make you wise for salvation through faith in Christ Jesus" (2 Tim. 3:15). Wisdom, then, comes through familiarity with God's Word.

If you claim to be a follower of Jesus Christ, yet you do not open your Bible with any regularity, if it is largely a strange book to you, this is not the mark of a disciple. If you are counting on the minister to tell you what it means, or for the weekly reading of a few passages in church as your connection to the Bible, this is wholly insufficient to bring you to maturity as a follower of Jesus. Disciples are those who love God's Word.

Disciples Want to Grow in His Image

As many have noted, followers of Jesus are not sinless, but they should sin less. This is another way of saying that part of being a disciple is to become more like him. Most of the letters of the New Testament are encouragements to become more like Jesus, to resist sin and evil, and to follow him with increasing devotion. This makes sense because these letters were written to people who were already Christians. It is critical to see this point: These encouragements are not given so that we might become Christians. They are given because the recipients already are Christians. A paraphrase might be, "You're now part of the family; act like it."

Paul wrote this to the Ephesians: "I therefore, a prisoner for the Lord, urge you to walk in a manner worthy of the calling to which you have been called, with all humility and gentleness, with patience, bearing with one another in love, eager to maintain the unity of the Spirit in the bond of peace" (Eph. 4:1–3). The qualities of humility, gentleness, patience, and love; these are things the Lord Jesus displayed when he was here on earth. This is what disciples are called to do: resemble Christ.

One of the things children do is to mimic what they see others doing. It is often their parents whom they watch and imitate. Paul may have had this in mind when he said, "Therefore be imitators of God, as beloved children" (Eph. 5:1). Since believers have joined God's family and become his children, we should imitate our heavenly father and display attitudes and desires that he displays. The struggle between who they were in Adam and who they now are in Christ means that growing into that likeness is not a straight line. There will be peaks and valleys, triumphs and defeats, yet it is something disciples want to pursue. If there is no desire to leave sin behind and to become more like the one who died for you, perhaps it means you are still holding on to a cultural faith, rather than true life.

Disciples Want to Magnify Christ

When disciples of John the Baptist came to him to tell him that people were flocking to Jesus, perhaps they thought to make him jealous. If so, they did not know him very well. John reminds them that he is not the Christ and that his whole ministry was to prepare the way for Jesus. "He must increase, but I must decrease" (John 3:30). John takes a place of submission to Jesus; he acknowledges that his service is all about making more of the Lord Jesus.

Making more of Jesus is in keeping with the purpose of God in the plan of salvation. Paul conveys this to the Ephesians when he writes that God "made known to us the mystery of His will, according to His kind intention which He purposed in Him with a view to an administration suitable to the fullness of the times, *that is*, the summing up of all things in Christ, things in the heavens and things on the earth" (Eph. 1:9–10 NASB). God has summed up everything in Christ. Disciples understand this and seek to enter into what God is doing.

God's purposes for this world are realized in Christ. He is literally God's final word to mankind. The writer of the epistle to the Hebrews begins by saying this:

> Long ago, at many times and in many ways, God spoke to our fathers by the prophets, but in these last days he has spoken to us by his Son, whom he appointed the heir of all things, through whom also he created the world. He is the radiance of the glory of God and the exact imprint of his nature, and he upholds the universe by the word of his power (Heb. 1:1–3).

In other words, God spoke to our forefathers in a variety of ways. He used prophets; he used dreams and visions, but now, late in history, he has spoken to us by his Son. After God sent his Son into the world, there was nothing further to say, no clearer message that he could give. Jesus is the culmination of all that God is doing and indeed has done. Because of this, disciples are those who echo this proclamation of the supremacy of Jesus.

Our personal fulfillment as people is not God's chief end. It is rather the glorification of his Son. But the upshot is this: We experience life to the fullest, life as God meant us to, when we take our place as followers of Jesus and turn from ourselves. By minimizing self, and maximizing Jesus, disciples experience a liberty that none but Christians know.

Disciples Want to See Others Born Again

At the end of Matthew's gospel is the Great Commission. Jesus instructs his followers to go out into all the world and make disciples. Followers of Jesus should multiply and tell others about him. As I've explained in previous chapters, this task has ironically become more difficult because so many people think they already know him, but they have embraced an imitation of the true gospel.

The widespread acceptance of these imitation gospels means that for many people, telling someone they are on the wrong road is considered rude and confrontational. However, look at what Jesus, the Prince of Peace, said:

> Do not think that I have come to bring peace to the earth. I have not come to bring peace, but a sword. For I have come to set a man against his father, and a daughter against her mother, and a daughter-in-law against her mother-in-law. And a person's enemies will be those of his own household (Matt. 10:34–36).

Our natural rebellion creates an animosity between those who have entered into God's family and those who have not. Peace with

God is available through the gospel of his Son, but it comes through repentance and faith, a turning from self and to God. Since this means eternal life, why would a believer not want to see others experience this life?

Do you have friends and family who show no sign whatsoever of having a relationship with the Lord Jesus, but you aren't bothered? Is what is most important to you that they are happy and healthy, even if they remain in their sin? If you haven't given much thought at all to their eternity, this likely betrays your belief in a cultural gospel. Things such as "love one another" or "God understands everyone is doing their best" may be your actual creed. Your friends and family don't need to try their best; they need forgiveness from the guilt of their sins. That forgiveness comes only through the new birth.

Disciples understand that the only way others will experience eternal life is by crossing over from death to life, and they have an earnest desire to see others make that journey. They know that it is ultimately very cruel to let someone go on believing a lie, especially when that lie is not harmless. The lie of the imitation gospels is one that will lead to eternal separation from God. The follower of Jesus wants to see others come into the light, be liberated, and experience the joy of being truly born again.

No one needs to be a public speaker to tell others about Jesus. Eloquence is not the point. When Peter and his fellow disciples began to proclaim salvation in Jesus, the Jewish authorities noted that they were "unlearned men." They tried to forbid them, but Peter said, "We cannot but speak of what we have seen and heard" (Acts 4:20). Anyone can similarly tell others about what they have seen and heard in the Bible. Telling others what they have experienced in being born again is something disciples do.

That Your Joy May Be Full

My wife has a friend who is a very enthusiastic golfer. She plays every day, practices all the time, and it seems she can't get enough of the game. But she wasn't always that way. Her husband is a casual golfer who for years tried to get her interested in playing. She could see no reason to try it; it all seemed utterly boring to her. But one day she did try, and she was hooked. From that point on, she couldn't get enough golf and was amazed at what she had been missing.

Perhaps you look upon what I've discussed in the prior chapters like this woman's previous attitude. Spending time reading the Bible, thinking about who God is, going to meetings of a local church or a home group—you don't see the attraction. To be honest, it all seems rather boring. Just as my wife's friend didn't know what she was missing, I suggest that your experience of God may be the same. I don't doubt that's the case for some, but it's also completely understandable.

To Know Joy, Our Capacity for God Must Increase

Athletes must spend time training. Mountain climbers must get accustomed to altitude. Climbing peaks in Colorado is one thing, where the elevation is about 14,000 feet, but taking on Mount Everest is another. The height of Everest is double that. The capacity for taking on such heights has to be developed. Similarly, we have to develop our capacity for God's truth and God's thoughts. We are simply not used to breathing "heavenly air," and our earthbound desires are unaccustomed to thinking on eternal things. Our thoughts about God and his truth are too much formed by the world around us, rather than by God's revelation in his Word. God told the prophet Isaiah, "For as the heavens are higher than the earth, so are my ways higher than your ways and my thoughts than your thoughts" (Isa. 55:9).

Athletes likewise have to watch their diet, because what they eat either translates into energy, or becomes a drag on their performance. For the Christian, the main course is always the Bible. Feeding on God's Word is essential to increasing our capacity to understanding God's truth. Paul tells Timothy, "As for you, continue in what you have learned and have firmly believed, knowing from whom you learned it and how from childhood you have been acquainted with the sacred writings, which are able to make you wise for salvation through faith in Christ Jesus" (2 Tim. 3:14–17). In other words, "Timothy, remember that I taught you the truth of God, and that truth is contained in the Scriptures. Keep your nose in that book, because it facilitates your growth; it empowers your understanding of salvation in Jesus Christ."

The other side of a good diet is to avoid empty calories. If we are to increase our capacity for God, we need to cut out the spiritual junk food that so much of our culture feeds on. It involves rejecting the errors of the imitation gospels I discussed previously. It is an unappreciated fact that spiritual harm comes to us in many ways, quite often from things that those around us find no problem with at all. Peter writes about the desires that his readers formerly pursued, but which "wage war against your soul" (1 Peter 2:11). Since becoming a Christian, is there anything of your former life you have become uncomfortable with? Is there anything you participated in before that you can no longer partake in? If the answer is no, it doesn't mean there is nothing warring against your soul. It means you are losing the war. If our capacity to understand and enjoy God is curtailed, it may be because we have a poor spiritual diet.

To Know Joy, We Must See Things from God's Perspective

If we do not experience the joy that the Scriptures promise to the redeemed, it is likely because we are untrained to see things from his point of view. One of the chief ways we gain that capacity is by a true assessment of what matters eternally. We are so used to what one writer has called the "tyranny of the urgent" that we forget that what truly matters is what will remain forever. Paul says, "The things that are seen are transient, but the things that are unseen are eternal" (2 Cor. 4:18).

The New Testament presents eternity as the thing we are preparing ourselves for. This life is brief and fleeting. Indeed, while we are on this earth, the Bible urges Christians to be good stewards of the time and resources we have been given, but it never sees this life as an ultimate goal and as something we cling to. The usual concerns people have—health, family, money—while they are real, are not eternal. The New Testament is clear that such things cannot take from believers what they have in Christ and who they are in Christ. When we instead focus our attention on the eternal, we begin to shape our hearts for what they are meant for.

In the upside-down value system that our culture promotes, we believe things like having enough money, being successful, or being comfortable—these are what matter. We want our circumstances to be good. But the Scriptures present two truths that are at odds with this. First, no promise is given to followers of Jesus that our circumstances will be comfortable or to our short-term advantage. In fact, the New Testament acknowledges the likely possibility that followers of Jesus will have difficult circumstances. Paul was beaten, arrested, shipwrecked, the target of attempted murder, and spent several years in prison—all because of his faith in Jesus. He invited his young charge Timothy to "suffer hardship with *me*, as a good soldier of Christ Jesus" (2 Tim. 2:3 NASB).

Second (and importantly), the New Testament also teaches that our circumstances cannot diminish anything of what God has promised to us. In fact, they may be used to increase our likeness to Jesus. Peter wrote to a group of scattered believers in Asia Minor to encourage them in their difficulties. "Though now for a little while, if necessary, you have been grieved by various trials, so that the tested genuineness of your faith—more precious than gold that perishes though it is tested by fire—may be found to result in praise and glory and honor at the revelation of Jesus Christ" (1 Peter 1:6–7).

God is using these trials, Peter says, as tools in his hands to refine our souls and to make us more like his Son here and now, before heaven. Being in comfortable circumstances is not God's ultimate purpose for believers in Jesus. Making them more like Jesus in their character and temperament is. When followers of Jesus get hold of this, and understand what God is doing, we begin to think his thoughts, and it brings a satisfaction like nothing the world offers.

Paul also testified that "I have learned in whatever situation I am to be content. I know how to be brought low, and I know how to abound. In any and every circumstance, I have learned the secret of facing plenty and hunger, abundance and need. I can do all things through him who strengthens me" (Phil. 4:11–13). The secret Paul learned was it is the Lord Jesus Christ who is the key to his sufferings having eternal value. If you have trouble seeing this, it could be because you have not learned what Paul learned. Your gaze is not focused in the distance, toward eternity.

When Capacity for God Grows, Satisfaction in Him Grows

The process of maturing in Christ brings its own reward. As we come to life spiritually, and understand all that God has done and is doing for us, it is like the blind being able to see for the first time. John Piper explains it this way:

> Once we had no delight in God and Christ was just a vague historical figure. What we enjoyed was food and friendships and productivity and investments and vacations and hobbies and games and reading and shopping and sex and sports and art and TV and travel . . . but not God. He was an idea—even a good one—and a topic for discussion; but He was not a treasure of delight. Then something miraculous happened. It was like the opening of the eyes of the blind during the golden dawn. First the stunned silence before the unspeakable beauty of holiness. Then the shock and terror that we had actually loved the darkness. Then the settling stillness of joy that this is the soul's end.[1]

Piper describes one whose joy and satisfaction are increasingly found in God. It is not so much what God has done for us in forgiving our sins and in granting us eternal life, but it is that he himself becomes our delight and contentment. Thankfulness for the pardon from sin is surely there, but the focus changes from the benefits to the benefactor. Christians through the ages have understood this and rejoiced to see it as God's work in their hearts. The things which once held our attentions, what we once sought and labored for, lose their hold on us. As the heart is transformed to be more like Christ, our joy in him increases.

Perhaps you doubt that such could ever be your experience, or you aren't sure you even want it to be your experience. Paul again has the answer. Ascribing praise to God he writes, "Now to him who is able to do far more abundantly than all that we ask or think, according to the power at work within us, to him be glory in the church and in Christ Jesus throughout all generations, forever and ever. Amen" (Eph. 3:20–21). As much as we can think of, God can do more. As rich and abundant as we may imagine God and his power to be, it is far more, says Paul. Our thoughts of God's omnipotence and power only touch the edges. As Job marveled, "These are but the outskirts of his ways" (Job 26:14).

Elsewhere, Paul has asked the question that if God has given us his own Son, "How will he not also with him graciously give us all things?" (Rom. 8:32). J. I. Packer helps us get the right perspective on this:

> Paul's "all things" is not a plethora of material possessions, and the passion for possessions has to be cast out of us in order to let the "all things" in. For this phrase has to do with knowing and enjoying God, and not with anything else. The meaning of "he will give us all things" can be put thus: one day we shall see nothing—literally nothing—which could have increased our eternal happiness has been denied us, and that nothing—literally nothing—that could have reduced that happiness has been left with us. What higher assurance do we want than that?[2]

We are sometimes like small children who don't understand what our parents are doing, why they are denying us some things and giving us others. Later, when we mature, we understand what they were doing. Packer is saying God is doing the same with us. God "has blessed us in Christ with every spiritual blessing in the heavenly places" (Eph. 1:3). Those in Christ lack nothing for their eternal good.

Though we live our lives in these bodies and on this earth, the ones made new in Christ are actually citizens of heaven now, at this moment! To understand and appreciate all this is to experience God's intention for believers. If you cannot see this, to paraphrase Paul, you don't know what you're missing. Cultural Christians inhabit this space of not knowing the blessings of being in Christ, being born again. I know this because I was in this position. I was one who, though I would never have said I didn't believe in God, I did not have the personal relationship that comes from the new birth. Myriads have had the same experience.

The assertions of cultural Christianity are a shallow pool compared to the depths of God's promises for those who are born again. Perhaps not overtly stated, the message of cultural faith is that your life can remain undisturbed—as you want it—and by completing some perfunctory obligations, such as being a good person and trying to be kind to others, you've done the things God asks. I've shown in the previous pages how none of this accords with the revealed truths of God's Word. God must disturb our lives to make them new. Apart from being made new, we cannot experience the joy of what it means to know Jesus.

A friend recently told me her story of moving from cultural faith to genuine trust in God. Mary had a typical Midwest upbringing. Her family attended a mainline church and her father was quite active, serving on various boards. When Mary was a teenager, a new minister came to the church. The previous minister had preached a kind of feel-good message that God loves us all and wants us to be happy. But the new minister began to talk about sin and the need to be born again. Hearing this message, Mary believed and put her trust in the Lord Jesus. She came home that night and told her father she had become a Christian. Her father was perplexed. "What do you mean? You've always been a Christian! I'm going to talk to that fellow."

Though it was late at night, Mary's father did indeed talk to the minister. He stayed for three hours, arriving home at 1 a.m. The next morning, he announced that he understood what the minister had said, and saw how he, too, needed to be saved.

Mary and her father experienced deliverance from a cultural faith that differed from what the Bible said. They saw themselves to be sinners in need of pardon and whose good lives were useless to provide that pardon or remove their guilt.

Like Mary and her father, you, too, can come out of darkness and into the light. Nothing of a good life can remove your guilt and bring you into God's family. Jesus alone, his death and resurrection, is the only thing acceptable to God for your pardon. Faith in God's Son as the Bible presents him—this is what brings you into his family. Why not take this step of faith today?

Afterword

It's a very difficult thing to encompass everything about the Christian life in a few pages. After all, the Bible is a book of 66 books that presents an unfolding story of God's redemptive plan beginning in Eden and ending with a new heaven and a new earth. There is a lot there! But what I have tried to do is show how the Bible speaks of what it means to enter into God's family, to cross over from death to life. If you've read these pages and recognized that what you thought about God and eternal life was based more on tradition or on the church culture you were raised with, and you've come to see you need to be born again, I would love to hear from you! A journey of knowing more about God and all that he has done for you through the Lord Jesus is a lifelong process. Cultivating that relationship and knowing God better through his Word are now among the things that await you. I hope your experience will be that you appreciate more and more the wonder of God's salvation; not just what he has done in making a way for you to be forgiven, but what he continues to do in drawing you to himself in greater intimacy.

If I can help you know God better, please contact me through my website: www.gentlemantheologian.com.

Notes

Chapter 1: Cultural Christianity
1. Pew Forum, "Religious Landscape Study," Pew Research Center, accessed April 19, 2019, http://www.pewforum.org/religious-landscape-study/.
2. *Merriam-Webster*, s.v. "nominal," accessed May 2, 2019, https://www.merriam-webster.com/dictionary/nominal?utm_campaign=sd&utm_medium=serp&utm_source=jsonld.
3. Pew Forum, "Religious Landscape Study," Pew Research Center, accessed April 19, 2019, http://www.pewforum.org/religious-landscape-study/.
4. "Christian Witness to Nominal Christians Among Protestants (LOP 23)," Lausanne Movement, accessed April 19, 2019, https://www.lausanne.org/content/lop/lop-23#1.

Chapter 2: Imitation Gospels
1. Alanna Petroff, "The 'Fakes' Industry Is Worth $461 Billion," CNN Business, April 18, 2016, http://money.cnn.com/2016/04/18/news/economy/fake-purses-shoes-economy-counterfeit-trade/index.html.

Chapter 3: God's Blueprint
1. Paul Little, "What Non-Christians Ask," accessed May 2, 2019, http://www2.wheaton.edu/bgc/archives/docs/little1.htm.
2. Timothy Keller, *The Reason for God: Belief in an Age of Skepticism* (New York: Riverhead Books, 2008), 8.
3. Ibid., 9.

Chapter 4: Missing the Mark
1. Geoffrey C. Ward, "The Veneer of Civilization," *The Vietnam War*, season 1, episode 7, directed by Ken Burns and Lynn Novik, aired September 25, 2017.

2. Jerry Bridges, *Respectable Sins: Confronting the Sins We Tolerate* (Colorado Springs: NavPress, 2007), 20–21.
3. Tim Challies, "God's Not Really That Holy, I'm Not Really That Bad," November 9, 2015, https://www.challies.com/articles/gods-not-really-that-holy-im-not-really-that-bad.

Chapter 5: The Love of God
1. D.A. Carson, *The Difficult Doctrine of the Love of God* (Wheaton, IL: Crossway Books, 2000), 11–12.

Chapter 6: The Wrath of God
1. John Blanchard, *Whatever Happened to Hell?* (Wheaton, IL: Crossway Books, 1995), 170.
2. A.W. Tozer, *The Knowledge of the Holy* (San Francisco: Harper and Row, 1961), 95.
3. Keller, *The Reason for God*, 75–76.

Chapter 7: Turning from Sin
1. Harry A. Ironside, *Except Ye Repent* (New York: American Tract Society, 1937), 189.
2. Trevin Wax, "The Mark of Christianity That Is Disappearing from Our Worship," August 27, 2015, https://www.thegospelcoalition.org/blogs/trevin-wax/the-mark-of-christianity-that-is-disappearing-from-our-worship.

Chapter 9: That Your Joy May Be Full
1. John Piper, *Desiring God: Meditations of a Christian Hedonist* (Portland: Multnomah Press, 2011), 71.
2. J. I. Packer, *Knowing God* (Downers Grove, IL: InterVarsity Press, 1973), 270.

www.ingramcontent.com/pod-product-compliance
Lightning Source LLC
Chambersburg PA
CBHW070628050426
42450CB00011B/3142